FOOTSTEPS OVER IMPERFECTION

A COMPILATION OF UNEMBELLISHED THOUGHTS IN THE FORM OF 51 POETRY

AARNA MALOT

I would like to dedicate this book to the two most supportive individuals of my life, my mom and dad. Every emotion, every expression and every element of these poetry, is wholly a result of their investment in my life. Infact, I believe I am able to write and appreciate literature only because of their interests. My dad, an avid reader and my mom, a story teller, have both exemplified the importance and understanding of literature and other forms of art. Without their encouragement none of this would have been possible.

A large part of this work, is also dedicated to my extended family, friends and acquitances. It is only because of their presence, that I have had varied experiences worth recording in my life.

Contents

Contents

Contents

Preface

Nothing is in a chronological order- both in my life and in my book.

For my first publication, I chose to record poetry I've written as a 13 year old and as a 17 year old. Everything written in these 51 poetry, reflects the most unembellished thoughts I have had in these few years. From descibing the characters in my life, to imaginary situations; from small impactful incidents, to deeply woven ideologies, this book comes out to be the amalgamation of every single idea I've had when I sat with a pen in my hand.

1. Window

Ahead of me there's a lot to see,
Of where to go and what to be.
But I like to view, what's now to mean,
Every moment, bright and free.
Where I can find my peace,
Find love, my every piece,
The other's find contempt,
To steal my eager ease.
It's all in what to see,
From the window in your lee,
A glittering green mountain,
Or a pink and purple sea.
You see, what you chose,
With that window open or close,
Red and raw velvety petals,
Or prickling thorns in a rose.
If the mountains you can view,
To scale new heights stirring and new,
Or feel frightened by a fall,
Your window represents you.
You think about what you've seen,
The grass is always lush and green.
Or there lies dirt beneath,

The window reflects who you've been.
It's all just the window.
The window of your mind you know.
Whether it's hazy, clear or calm,
It makes you out of what it shows.

2. Party Politics

In high school halls, where whispers brew,
Cliques form fast, dividing the crew,
Girls in clusters, alliances tight,
In the dance of popularity, they ignite,
Labels thrown like confetti in the air,
As they weave through the maze of who's "fair."
One group reigns supreme, crowned in glory,
Their power, a narrative, a well-worn story,
Others watch from the sidelines, feeling small,
Excluded, they navigate the social sprawl,
Their voices drowned in the din of exclusion,
In this party of politics, a cruel illusion.
The queen bees buzz with their chosen few,
While others languish in the shadows' hue,
Behind fake smiles, lies a world of pain,
As they endure the sting of disdain,
In this microcosm, where acceptance is rare,
They seek solace in the hope of repair.
But change is slow, and scars run deep,
In this realm where appearances keep,
Yet amidst the chaos, seeds of defiance sow,
As they refuse to bow to the status quo,
For in unity lies the strength to defy,

The party politics that make some cry.

3. Footsteps Over Imperfection

Even when the brightest sun shines,
The prettiest stars begin to twinkle.
Christmas markets sparkle,
And bells begin to jingle.
She still walks home,
That mere brown stick.
Faded clothes, bare hands,
Black glasses and face toned.
She never spoke a single word,
Never smiled, never heard.
Her shadows faded into her abode,
That no man had ever known.
Maybe she had a fierce ego,
Maybe she let her happiness go.
Or drank immense arrogance,
Something's killed her eloquence.
And back and forth,
She went for a penny,
Not a single partner,
Not a single ally.
So let her die,
In her own world.

When there's nothing she bothered,
Why should we wonder?
But listen you blind world!
Stop your looping speculations.
When there's so much in your view,
Why don't you see, that she can't see?
Where a million colours,
You say, you have.
She has her own colour,
A unique perception.
Let her build, her own world.
These are her footsteps over imperfection.

4. Within

I was flowing all about,
In the unpredictable vicissitudes.
To myself I was unknown,
To all the world, I was unknown!
For what I did, why I did?
My image was a mystery,
And so was my desire.
But a little I did replenish,
And so did my surroundings.
I thought it was them, who did,
Changed my crude broken bits.
But little did I know, the change was within,
Slowly awakening, understanding did begin.
In the quiet of reflection, in moments of calm,
I saw myself clearer, like a soothing balm.
Not the world nor others, but my own hand,
Molded the clay of my fate, as I began to understand.
The vicissitudes still dance, the unknown yet vast,
But I navigate now, with purpose unveiled at last.

5. A Little Man

There I stood, among the many.
One voice, among the plenty.
Cheering, screaming, laughing, crying,
Among a thousands, I was trying.
Trying to take a glimpse of him.
Praying for him, his times were grim.
A man whose image was larger than life,
For who I could always strife.
A moment, he walked on the green span.
I stopped and noticed a little man.
For who I thought, how lovely was he,
After all he was just like me.
A man who seemed so ordinary.
In my life became extra-ordinary.
For it wasn't his wealth, name and fame.
It was just how naturally he played life's game.

6. Popularity Contest

High school began,
And so did the popularity contest.
Who was handsome?
And who was the smartest?
Somehow I topped it,
Without even participating.
I was good at singing,
Academics and debating.
But oh what sorrow!!
Why did I win??
Acquaintances were jealous,
Their egos were thin.
It was fun to be familiar,
And to talk to new people.
But I had to be perfect,
My attitude- feeble.
For a notorious kid like me,
It seemed almost impossible.
To be well mannered,
And say things plausible.
And popularity isn't all things glorious,
It can be mean and difficult.
On the top of your game,

Your mind can feel exult.
To be famous isn't the same as fake,
To be appreciated, people need to relate.
If you are natural, it doesn't matter,
Whether you can sing, dance or debate.
All I learnt, I shouldn't be ashamed.
Of who I am now, how it came?
All it takes, is to be nice and fair,
Don't insult, don't defame.

7. A Table Lamp

I saw her little fingers,
Obstructing my way to the letter.
She wrote like another crazy.
A day active, another lazy.
With time, I grew with her,
And testing times were.
For I saw the white plain,
A little moist in pain.
Jolly hours came,
when problems seemed lame,
And finished them in a heap
And she put me to quick sleep.
Sometimes I saw pictures,
Of cars or water pitchers.
Someday colourful sticks,
Or a bottle to fix.
Her faults came my way,
Inputs I wanted to say.
But I never spoke,
To my lovely folk.
We met every day, sure.
My life was what for?
She was my life's right,

And I was her life's light.
My absence was her fear,
Together we were every year.
Our friendship didn't revamp,
She called me "A Table Lamp"

8. The Sunshine on my Settee

In a sanctuary earned through toil,
Where light dances with fragrance's coil.
A haven bespoke, solely mine,
Adorned with teal and white's design.
Literary comrades by my side,
Humor's jesters, ever allied.
Stretch of velvet, plush and grand,
With loving arms, oh so grand.
Above, ropes of glimmering grace,
'Neath sheer drapes, a soft embrace.
Each dawn, I would gently bypass,
For treasures rare, as morn did pass.
The Sunshine on my Settee, sparkles like liquid gold,
An unreplacable warm hug, on twilights cold.
A vision fair, a soul's true delight,
In this space, bathed in daylight's might.

9. Words Seldom Written

It's all in the words,
You seldom write,
A sense of gratitude,
Felt dynamite.
The practice of your presence,
And contentment in you,
And often acceptance,
Of something you value.
Like the creatures in our wild,
Were abundant in style.
And no man cared,
To save it for a while.
When bid there "byes",
Of struggle they die.
Campaigns and cares,
Save a penny to defy.
Like rich men's boys,
With plates full and toys,
He often abuses,
Ill-treats his wealthy alloys.
But only when, a poor kid,
Begs at his window,
He empties the plates,

And cuddles his pillow.
Like a pretty woman,
In the wealthy courts,
Who flaunts her beauty,
For jolly dollar notes.
But only when she's asked,
To be a dance girl,
She shamefully takes,
Her pride for a swirl.
Like stars in the dark,
A decade ago.
Myriad and majestic,
Plenty and more.
But only when the dirt,
And dust hid them all,
Little kids count and,
Ask where are they gone?
It's all in the words,
We seldom write.
A sense of gratitude
Felt dynamite.
It's more of presence,
Than a heartfelt "thank-you".
More of an acceptance,
Of something you'll value.

10. Four Bottles of Stars

A long time ago,
I saw a beautiful sight.
A sight so magical,
That brought me to light.
Four bottles of stars,
All hung together.
With beautiful golden tops,
Like mystical heather.
And every crystal bottle,
Had stars of a different colour.
While two were sparkling bright,
The other two were duller.
Each one on themselves,
Was dulcet and fine.
An individual character,
Power, peace and divine.
Solely they told a story,
Of their own influence.
From where they came,
And what was their very essence.
But what a serendipity!
Now they were a bunch.
A bunch so striking and serene,

That carried a secret hunch.
However varied we might be,
We are precious in our own way.
And when we come together,
The world is better each day.
Colour, shape and place,
Don't have to always divide.
You embrace and celebrate them,
They can even bring and bind.
Once your bond's made,
It'll heal all your scars,
And you'll be as beautiful,
As the four bottles of stars.

11. Hidden Silence

On a lonely road,

When you walk carefree,

The trees, the crickets,

Sing a song,

Amidst the night.

The branches and leaves,

Like pain would crackle.

But, you'll find a hidden silence.

By the green lake,

When you fiddle with the pebbles,

The water, the ripples,

And the land,

Will whisper a secret.

And even in the slightest dawn,

You'll find a hidden silence.

On the terrace,

Under the soothing light,

The stars, the moon,

And the wind,

Will giggle quietly.

And even in the darkest night,

You'll find a hidden silence.

12. Tomboy Type

Super lazy to dress,
Yet doesn't fail impress.
Typical ambivert personality,
Carefree, playful mentality.
Intolerant towards labrish,
She's humorous and savage.
Hates the "heel culture"
Ain't a complexity lover.
Got nice and long hair,
Seldom allowed to flair.
No parties, no dances,
Favourite word- nonsense.
Adventurous and tough.
Likes to play it rough,
Can totally intimidate,
With an unplanned debate.
Hates the fancy media,
Funnily wants to join collegia.
Generous and kind,
Soft-hearted on the hind.
Although more detached,
Her emotions are patched.
She's got an unmatched vibe,

Classified as the "Tomboy Type"

13. Roadside

A Sunday afternoon,
The sun was no festoon.
I soon had to make a move,
So I stood on my hooves.
A bustling roadside pathway,
I just wanted to go away.
For the noise so annoyed me,
It almost urged me to flee.
Something then just caught my eye,
Something I couldn't deny.
That taught me a lesson,
Worth more than a million.
A poor little child, begged and cried,
For sweet goodies, baked and fried.
His even poorer mother, without a penny,
For her hungry child, felt pity.
Just there when I looked aside,
Stood a pretty girl beside.
Who fed her prettier puppies,
Some sweet and salty goodies.
Then the puppies shockingly stopped,
To eat the goodies, for which they hopped.
And looked towards the hungry child,

Became silent, soft and mild.
With hopeful eyes, they saw their lady,
And truly knew she wasn't shady.
Their hope melted her gentle heart,
Merely urged her to do her part.
She bought plenty goodies from the roadside,
Sweet and hot, baked and fried.
And gave it to the craving child,
Whose little smile, couldn't hide.
The joy on his innocent face,
Brought happiness and solace.
To the seller, to his mother,
To the puppies and their mother.
But to me, who silently saw,
This small incident in awe,
Joy and content cam so strong,
With a lesson to remember lifelong.

14. One Way

God created just one way,
To pure and sole happiness.
Just one encounter,
And it'll brighten your day.
This way, I'll tell you.
Is the most puissant, among all.
It's presence is so sanguine,
And love it spreads true.
It provides lives,
To rich and poor alike.
It empowers bodies,
For strength it strives.
It connects souls,
With its language of love.
It builds families,
With people of different roles.
It brings back togetherness,
To whom have parted ways.
It brings back emotions,
To whom have lost tenderness.
It celebrates and welcomes,
A good deal of beings.
It provides comfort,

Even when one trembles.
It provides a living,
To everyone in its journey.
It bestows a blessing,
To each one preparing and giving.
Now my friend, I'm sure you brood,
What's this way? Where to go?
This way I tell you, is nothing,
But a simple plate of food.

15. The Shore Lore

I stare at the shore,
More and more.
And I wonder why,
It is so shy.
I look at it, it turns away,
I chase it, it swirls to play.
Its waves come close to me,
So transient! They revert back to the sea.
Oh please! Don't go away.
Just listen to what I say.
My feet in the wet sand,
Your soft touch in my hand,
So palpable, so desperate,
To forget all contempt and hate!
Then the cold water's breeze,
Provides to me, unlaboured ease.
You, me and the evening sky.
The orange sun bids a bye.
And the expanse so dark and dense,
No one is around us, hence,
You come back to me,
Fear you'll be lonely.
Hurry up! I need to go,

Tell me the lore, quite and slow.
Every time I meet the shore,
I fall for it, more and more.
And I wonder why,
It is so shy.
I go away, it pleads to stay.
I turn back, its ready to play.
Its waves come close to me,
Sigh! I know they belong to the sea.

16. Album of My Mind

Rise a day, hazy sunlight.
Windy grasslands, spirits alive.
Bluish play, pebbles around,
Silent chatter, peaceful ground.
Dancing dandelions, whispering trees,
Carefree grasslands, among the breeze.
Happy wings, quite minds,
Flying hair, feet that binds.
This is the only sight,
The only one to remind.
Of my gratitude and my might,
The one picture in the album of my mind.

17. The Phone Call

The phone call you made,
On a dry march evening,
Was for sure, I'm afraid,
Of full intentional meaning.
Furious I was not,
Rather felt dubiety and disappointment.
Your words were jealousy fraught,
Like your insecurity's ointment.
"Oh! How lovely would it be,
To share", I thought.
But your ego was set free,
I brutally forgot.
What a beautiful exhibition,
I saw of your character.
Your poisonous affliction,
Couldn't stand my nectar.
The exposed reality,
Made you blatantly laugh.
Your heart was a malady,
And trust was half.
And if a little failure,
Your manhood can't take.
You've watched the trailer,

Without a futile break.
Furious I am not,
Rather hurt and disappointed.
Over the misery I got,
With what a boy did.

18. Granny's Veranda

That morning oil massage,
Under the Jasmine tree,
Where the sun shone in patches,
During the winter spree.
Her gentle hands on my forehead,
For more time, I would plea.
Out in the veranda,
Early in the evenings,
She'd feed me summer fruits,
And share her homely feelings.
Her aged voice sang sweetly,
To me and my siblings.
Before bed time,
She assembled us back in the porch.
This time to tells us,
Tales of Gods and demiurge.
And sometimes her childhood stories,
To tell us, we would urge.
Granny's Veranda,
White and green memories.
Mangoes and crisps,
Pickles and peas.
Endless conversations,

AARNA MALOT

Forgotten worries.

19. Who Knew It'd be This Hard?

People have always said,
"success requires sacrifice",
But until one doesn't try,
One doesn't realise.
It's a painful truth,
For the ambitious youth.
Suddenly to me,
My dreams seem expensive.
They demand my energy,
And discipline extensive.
Destroying my smaller goals,
They snatched away my awaited roles.
Wanted to be School President,
All of a sudden, I can't.
For singing and dancing,
No permission grant.
Every fun day with my friends,
Came to an unfortunate end.
No, I am not unhappy about,
Giving up on things I like.
Obviously, I wish to see,
My dreams and life alike.

AARNA MALOT

But, life didn't give a warning card,
Who knew it'd be this hard?

20. Ample Hero

Incomparable intelligence,
Beyond brilliantly bright,
He isn't a common man,
Knows what's wrong and right.
Assiduous towards academics,
Excellence- appreciator.
He listens and observes,
And is an outspoken leader.
Achiever he is for sure,
Yet humbled and kind.
Serious on the front side,
Humorous on the hind.
Generous and grateful,
He is a wonderful son.
Unusually supportive,
Makes his wife have fun.
Inspirational and admirable,
Ego level zero.
My father unquestionably,
To me is ample hero.

21. For A Little While

Let me be myself,
Let me be alone,
Let me desperate,
For a little while.
Give me some freedom,
Give me some grace,
Give me wings to fly,
For a little while.
Leave my wrists,
Leave my eyes open,
Leave me to escape this town,
For a little while.
Forgive my ignorance,
Forgive my goofiness,
Forgive my patience for you,
For a little while.
Handle my insanity,
Handle my barefaced behaviour,
Handle my ambitious breakthrough,
For a little while.
I'll be alright!
I'll survive!
Allow my crudity to thrive,

For a little while.

22. Craters

The big white globe,
In the dark, a glow.
When the awake has slept,
Its reticence has crept.
A symbol of beauty,
Feminine glory.
Impeccably powerful,
Sparks wonderful.
One step behind,
Better complacency to find.
No blemish, no splotch,
So spectacular like scotch.
The craters are there,
Witty and aware.
An unspoken issue,
A worn out tissue.
The glamour is confident,
The sight is bent.
The foible is forgotten,
The memory is golden bottom.
Craters are inexorable,
Disgust can turn adorable.
The play is of the charisma,

A day a sphere, another a prisma.

23. No Degree

Every accomplishment, ever made,
Was valuable only for a grade.
Whether one was first, or the best,
Or one's score in a test.
To accept one or to agree,
All that matters is his degree.
And another important thing you know,
Is the qualification you own.
But for you to be a good man,
There's no degree, no scan.
Before falling in love with one,
Does the other question, on what one's done?
Does a child, before being born,
Asks what gems his parents adorn?
And do parents not love their baby,
Because he doesn't have a resume' fancy?
Does a man ask God for his list of awards,
To accept him as his Lord?
Or does God not bless them who,
Small and pity works do?
In true sense, there's no degree,
For one to be happy and free.
It's just what one seeks to see,

The heart, the mind or the glee.

24. Dear Richard

Every morning, down the hallway,
His winsome laughter started the day.
Teacher's favourite, helped juniors study,
Seniors' confidant, was my buddy.
He was kind, he was brave,
He had all the love to save.
The drums he played and the guitar.
He won every person's heart.
"Who doesn't know Richard?"
In every classroom was heard.
The one mate we all wanted,
I had taken him for a little granted.
He was beyond generous to me,
When I cried, made me happy.
He taught me and scolded too,
In the canteen, got me fondue.
Deep down there, for him I cared.
But to express, I never really dared.
He was so selfless and true,
With time passing, our friendship grew.
They say the precious are gone too soon,
Before I knew, he left for the moon.
Too-too away, so-so far,

And I was left with a huge scar.
Dear Richard forgive me,
If I've ever been rude or mean.
Come back down, oh please do!
I promise I'll bring you fondue.
This time I'll make you cards,
Sing all the songs you starred.
You can scold and not talk to me,
But, a man like you can never be.

25. 7:49 PM

Thank heavens she texted me at 7:49 PM,
And obscurely shared that she had reached the end.
There's a strange satisfaction in how I see,
My one real person, suddenly set free.
Though close we are, we're more detached,
With one good-bye our strings are re-patched.
We ask no questions and demand on replies,
On silence and acceptance our bare trust lies.
It's oddly pleasing to see her blurt,
Of how bravely she fought that hurt.
Feels I've re-won someone who is already mine,
A brand new furnish to a friendship fine.
Though seeking validation wasn't my thing,
I'm not guilty of how it's working.
Grateful we are for 7:49 PM.
Atleast we're both happy in the end.

26. Sunflower

He is a sunflower,
Among the daffodils.
A subtle element,
In the hushed hills.
Between the very whites,
He is a winsome yellow.
With energy and charisma,
That come humble and mellow.
The soil, the greens,
And the sky are his friends.
His smile is graceful,
So are his intends.
With the zephyr,
He dances and sways.
May the lord protect him,
The universe prays.

27. Last Whisper

That day was a note,
Like something unknown.
An awaited time, awaited result,
For which, like a clock I worked.
The morning was caught,
A little anxious and distort.
The twilight was fine,
But a desperate mind,
Was hid by a smile.
Discomfited were the eyes.
Beyond capacity, beyond control,
Emotions just flowed and flowed.
The time arrived, bitter that ever,
Full fought battle, barely won.
I am broken, I am done,
Was just the last whisper.

28. Geopolitics is Painful

I've been reading a lot of Geopolitics lately,
My childhood favourite subject was History.
For some reason I was always interested,
How people in freedom and liberty were invested.
How they fought, how they believed,
How the leaders corrupt minds were revealed.
Determined minds, strong demands,
New laws, amendments and remands.
Lives sacrificed, poverty and drought,
Protests conducted, defaulters caught.
Fallen governments, public uprising,
Common-man opinions deciding.
Now I've grown and newly realised,
Those times were grey and demised.
In a moment, that's thought and gainful,
I have known, Geopolitics is painful.
Families are broken, dreams are destroyed.
Deceitful and mendacious methods deployed.
War and misery corrupts the generation,
Old and young experience frustration.
News and drama of conflicts seem fancy,
Until we discern the uncanny.
Real human evolution comes from love and brotherhood.

Compassion and well-framed ideas understood.

• 47 •

29. Amalfi Coast Reverie

Along the scenic Gulf of Solerno's grace,
I find solace in a leisurely embrace.
Where maidens on bicycles glide with ease,
And vendors sell blooms in a fragrant breeze.
The aroma of lemons, bright and bold,
Mingles with freshly baked focaccia sold,
A celebration of Europe's charm,
In this coastal haven, a soothing balm.
With gelato in hand and tote bag swung,
I wander amidst houses brightly hung,
Against the backdrop of the azure sea,
A picturesque scene, serene and free.
In bustling alleys, lively and quaint,
Cheerful crowds add to the vibrant paint,
This Italian panorama of joy unfurled,
A reverie in Amalfi, my favorite world.
Of all my travels, aspirations high,
Amalfi Coast's allure makes my heart sigh.

30. Swift Like Stories

Somebody once told me,

That our lives in recollection,

Seem to be Swift Like Stories.

Where men are mean,

In our quests of perfection.

Fantasies appear to be throbbing,

And disconnection from oneself,

Is a common phenomenon.

Reason-less sobbing,

Comes with cursing yourself.

You are transported to a character's life,

And apologise for unseen errors.

Relationships are fragile,

With your friends, family and wife.

You'll face reclusive terrors.

Some days you'll yearn for respect,

At times you'll beg for freedom.

Jealousy and mockery,

Will be experienced in different aspects.

But, you'll finally find your kingdom.

Living Swift Like Stories,

Will make you brave and fine.

Confusions and heart-breaks,

Empty lies and worries,
Will no more make you whine.
Self-satisfaction attainment,
Earthly nature appreciation,
Will slowly make it to you.
You'll be your own entertainment,
Without reputation depreciation.

31. Math Class

Let me introduce you,
To my one old nemesis.
Whether old or new,
I never fail to make a mess.
Math class for me,
Has always been a disaster.
Either my teacher is angry,
Or I have been talking faster.
Right after lunch break,
I'm mostly 10 minutes late.
My attendance is on stake,
Yet I'm playful with my fate.
When I've understood a lesson,
My homework isn't done.
And during a bewildering session,
Bench mate and I are having fun.
Somehow, I don't know how?
On surprise test days,
I take a holiday, ciao!
Issues follow in multiple ways.
I am guilty of copying assignments,
And without fail I borrow protractors.
But I earnestly attend assessments,

And I don't have test contractors.
Regardless of all these mishaps,
Math class has been fruitful.
Joyous and mischievous recaps,
And grades and scores handful!

32. Future Lawyers Alliance

Mad in the mind, strict in appearance,
Cold British humour, dull-lit ambience.
Papers, books and documents, all on the table.
Clicking pens, flipping pages, all available.
Mental analysis, rigorous discussions,
Big, bad conference, understanding repercussions.
Left-wing standards, right-wing views,
Quick questioning of what's in the news.
Funnily enough we're all in defiance.
Secretly made a Future Lawyers Alliance.
Serious and silly both at one time,
Flourish an openly argumentative enzyme.
Each's been to the Model United Nations,
Ironically believe, we commiserate with international
relations.
Though conscience and coffee are always present,
Legitimacy and rationality are often absent.
Opposition and statements are our reliance,
We've together fallen into a dangerous alliance.

33. Harley is in a Delusion

It's true, it's not easy to deal,
With first time rejection.
Unfortunately, Harley is in a delusion.
She was an over-achiever,
Born with a silver spoon in her mouth.
Everyone's favourite, without a doubt.
A fine violinist and a sprinter,
Nearly best-looking, city's illustrious.
Her streak of success, almost mysterious.
For the first time in her existence,
She's met fresh failure.
Ever unmet, ever unfamiliar.
No, she can't cope.
Now, hurt and traumatised.
She has failed her expectations, she just realised.
Instead of acceptance,
She has resorted to delusion.
Nobody on earth than her, has a better solution.
Who will tell poor Harley,
That fate isn't invariably kind?
Ups and downs are normal, who will remind?

34. Secondary Situation

Grown enough with a bright mind.
Ofcourse I know how I feel.
How troubles keep the entry alive,
Is ofcourse, I don't know how to deal.
Fist fights and combats aren't the issue,
But emotions and thoughts are.
In the secondary situation,
My emotions are moving far.
"Zero people energy" and ignorance,
Are different with the attitude.
The first is simple serenity,
The latter is considered mean and rude.
Damn the secondary situation!
My mind feels happier than ever.
There's a refreshing freedom,
From the forces cunning and clever.
The silence in my ideas,
And stability in my reactions,
Has brought back together,
My intelligence and vulnerability in a fraction.

35. Why I Loved Iron Man

In the heart of marvel, a legend born,
In steel, he crafted his heroic morn.
A knight in armour, with wit so keen,
In every battle, a triumphant scene.
With courage ablaze, his spirit did soar,
In Tony Stark's tale, I found love's core.
With genius mind, he forged his fate,
A beacon of hope, amidst the state.
Through trials dire, he stood unbroken,
His resolve like iron, never token.
In his flaws, a humanity so pure,
In Iron Man's saga, my love found allure.
With every flight, he reached the sky,
Defying odds, he'd never comply.
In crimson glow, he faced the night,
A guardian fierce, in armour bright.
His legacy etched in stars above,
In Iron Man's embrace, I found love.
Though battles waged, and darkness fell,
His light shone bright, a tale to tell.
In sacrifice, his essence bared,
A hero's heart, forever dared.

In every beat, his legacy's drum,
In loving Iron Man, I found home.

36. Overambitious

Expectations in my life are a paradox,
With myself, they are soaring high,
With the others, there super orthodox.
Somehow its all trying to breathe alive.
There's too much I require,
And miniscule amount of myself, I appreciate.
Sometimes wild and fiery is my desire.
A slight failure, and I depreciate.
It's like I keep chiseling myself,
In an urge to find the perfect edge.
Consolation awards can't sit on my shelf,
Only successes, I pledge.
"Don't be overambitious" I often hear,
It isn't easy to abruptly adapt.
Compromise and fiasco, I fear,
It's a vicious circle, and I am trapped.
It's an overwhelming state of being,
Where everything needs to seem right.
Elements understated are ceasing,
And easy acceptance is a fight.
But a single moment of exquisiteness,
Provides uncomparable satisfaction.
Although being arty is unquestionably a mess,

The joy it provides, is an irresistable attraction.

37. Fine Glass Mirror

She grants me freedom, boundless and true,
Allows my dreams to take their due.
Sensitive soul, so caring and kind,
In her pureness, solace I always find.
In the mirror of my mother's eyes,
I see a reflection, clear and wise.
Supportive whispers in the breeze,
Guiding me through life's uncertainties.
Her honesty, a fine glass mirror,
Reflects the truth, makes it clearer.
In her embrace, I find my way,
With every word, she lights my day.
With every decision, she stands by,
Embracing me, never asking why.
My mother's love, an eternal light,
Guiding me through the darkest night.
In the fine glass mirror of her grace,
I see my worth, in every trace.
For she reveals my true reflection,
In her loyalty, I find perfection.

38. Ambivert Conversion

In bustling halls, she once found delight,
Brimming with energy, a beacon so bright.
But now, a shift, a subtle retreat,
From the clamor of voices, she finds her seat,
In the quiet corners, her solace complete.
From the heart of the party to the edges she strays,
A quiet observer in the dimming of days.
The chatter that once fueled her soul,
Now overwhelms, takes its toll.
In solitude's embrace, she finds control.
Caught in the midst of a silent debate,
Between the extroverted past and the introverted fate.
She grapples with the tug-of-war inside,
As her once vibrant spirit begins to hide,
In the shadows, she seeks a place to confide.
With each passing day, she unravels anew,
Discovering depths in the solitude she grew.
No longer defined by the noise around,
In the silence, her true self is found,
In this ambivert journey, she's homeward bound.
Through the highs and lows, she learns to cope,
Navigating the balance, finding her hope.
No longer confined by societal norms,

She embraces her essence in quiet storms,
In this realistic tale, she transforms.

39. In a Wordless World

Life would be silent,
Communication would be peaceful.
Talents would go violent
And descriptions would turn stressful.
Amongst the people, intends would thrive.
Amongst the animals, expressions would talk.
Even in disappointment, no-one would strife,
Life would seem like the play of knock-knock.
There would be no scope for misunderstandings.
Excuses and explainations would be irrelevant.
Not a man would know of new findings,
And literature would be a non-existant element.
Songs and stories would lose all meaning,
No means to deliver discomfort.
Living looks unimaginable but interesting,
In a Wordless World.

40. Security Deposit

In the cosmic bank of fate, a deposit made,
Not in gold or silver, but in actions laid.
Each deed, a coin in the karmic vault,
Determining the course of life's intricate assault.
With every kindness shown, a dividend earned,
In the ledger of destiny, its pages turned.
For the currency of karma knows no deceit,
It echoes back the echoes of each heartbeat.
Like a shield against the storms of time,
Karma stands, a fortress sublime.
Guarding against the winds of fate,
It keeps the balance of life's intricate state.
For what you sow, you shall reap in kind,
In the tapestry of destiny, your actions bind.
So let kindness be your currency,
And compassion your eternal indemnity.
In the ledger of life, let your deeds be pure,
For in them lies the ultimate cure.
With every act of love and grace,
Secure your future in karma's embrace.
So let not fear nor doubt hold sway,
For karma's security lights your way.
In the symphony of existence, let it be said,

Your life is secured by the deeds you've spread.

• 65 •

41. Can Somebody Explain Why?

It hurts when somebody leaves, without explanations.

It seems impossible to cope, with changes irreversible.

One trembles tearing up, looking at old photographs.

One frantically laughs, reminiscing silly situations.

Moments of loss, impinge unexplainably.

Moments of gain, exhilarate unmeasurably.

Somedays a man is ashamed for what's done.

Somedays a man feebly forgives himself.

Times come ,when our dear ones seem jealousy frought.

Times come, when people around us seem impeccable.

Can Somebody Tell me Why God filled us with emotions?

Can Somebody Tell me Why humans experience confusion?

We do learn lessons, we do take notes,

We do repeat mistakes, We do everything again.

All these tumultous intensties certainly create impact.

Can Somebody Tell me Why so much is required?

42. Since 2007

I've been writing my tales, Since 2007.

I've been sixteen, I've been eleven.

My evolution as an individual surprises me,

Old fascinations have turned enemies.

I've turned a blind eye to multiple humiliations,

And I've kicked myself for baseless relations.

Now, when I look back, it appears to be witless,

I've grown up to be bold and reckless.

I tried to impress and seek valiadation,

From contemporaries who lacked reputation.

Now I don't even approach them for a talk,

I've flourished much above them for a shock.

I've said things I probably shouldn't have,

Experienced the repercussion of a gaffe.

Luckily enough, I've faced embarassment,

In the present, nothing feels to be an appeasement.

My styles have changed, I've gotten more subtle.

Perspectives and ideas are in a huddle.

Although more serious, I am taking it easy.

More of a workaholic disease.

I've been executing, changing and spectating, Since 2007.

Still anticipating the events of 2047.

But, It seems so attractive to perform the present.

Uninformed of what could be portent.

43. Agatha's Landscapes

In worlds of ink, where shadows dance,
Agatha's tales, they pull me in, entranced.
Mysteries woven with cunning flair,
Each page a journey, beyond compare.
From Hercule Poirot's sharp wit,
To Miss Marple's observations, lit,
In labyrinthine plots, they tread,
Where every clue, a thread.
With every twist, my mind's ensnared,
In her stories, I am ensconced, prepared,
For revelations that shock and surprise,
As secrets unravel before my eyes.
In quaint English villages, or on the Nile's shore,
Agatha's landscapes, I do explore,
Through her words, I roam far and wide,
In worlds where truth and deceit collide.
Oh, the fantasies her novels inspire,
Of sleuthing feats, to never tire,
To solve mysteries with prowess keen,
In a world where the truth is unseen.
So here's to Agatha, the master of suspense,
Whose tales leave me in utter recompense,
For in her novels, I find delight,

In fantasies that take flight, in the dead of night.

44. Some Temperament Brews

In every heart, some temperament brews,
A blend of hues, both bright and dark,
Yet in this symmetry, there's no taboo,
For each soul dances its unique spark.
Some wear their pride as a shining crown,
A regal stance, never bowing down.
Their confidence, a beacon in the night,
Guiding them through every daunting plight.
Others harbor a storm within,
A tempest raging, beneath the skin.
Their anger flares, a fiery blaze,
Yet it's passion that fuels their days.
Some souls are draped in a cloak of fear,
Their insecurities whispering near.
But in their vulnerability, there lies strength,
For bravery blooms at any length.
And then there are those with hearts of gold,
Whose kindness shines, a tale retold.
Their empathy, a balm for the soul,
Mending wounds to make us whole.
So let us embrace these temperaments diverse,
For in acceptance, we find our universe.

Each trait, a thread in humanity's weave,
A testament to what we believe.

45. Quite Loud

In a world ,where silence often reigns,
He stood apart, his voice unchained.
Opinions bold, thoughts uncontained,
Though many scoffed, he remained the unstained.
His words, like thunder, shook the ground,
Through criticism, his resolve was found.
Unyielding spirit, with wisdom crowned,
In the chaos, his truth resound.
Misunderstood by the timid crowd,
Yet his voice echoed strong and proud.
With every word, a vision avowed,
In the wilderness, he forged his shroud.
Through the storm of doubt, he pressed,
His convictions stronger than the rest.
In adversity, he found his quest,
His voice, a beacon, at its best.
Success adorned him, in due time,
For he dared to speak against the mime.
His loudness, not a flaw, but a paradigm,
A testament to courage, in its prime.
So let his tale inspire those who fear,
To speak their truths, loud and clear.
For in the symphony of voices, sincere,

Lies the power to triumph, persevere.

46. Headphones On my Soul

Listening what the nature wishes to convey,

In manifested stillness and convinced calm,

In the woods, where the concrete is away,

And the birds are our unpaid alarms.

The water - effervescent yet soothing,

The grass - jabbing yet comforting.

My idea and thoughts are in total absence,

All my sensory organs put to total activity.

The brain and the heart take chances,

To feel poised and on its ultimate relativity.

Feels like I've worn Headphones On my Soul.

Everything in me is quite yet there's so much talking to

whole.

These substances connect me to myself,

Agreements and disgreements internally are full-fledged.

My self-sufficing areas are found, and where I need help,

Recultance is re-tested where my behaviour is hedged.

With time passing by, uncomplications commence.

The gratification and solace are immense.

47. Mephistopheles

In the story of every Faust, there's a Mephistopheles.
To bring out rage and furity, resulting in anomalies.
In every making of a truly brave Wallace,
A Murray and his evils played a part in the place.
To the superhuman agility and loyalty of Thor,
Loki's cunningness and trickery roar.
For a devilish of a man like Sisyphus to be a paladin,
To an evil spirit like Lucifer, turned into an assasin.
In the Ramayana, the pious Ram became a legend,
Unholy Ravana was killed and reckoned.
The evil and the good have always coexisted,
The goodness and humanity have always persisted.
The satan is sure to die sooner or later,
Whether he is cruel or a traitor.
The saint shall rule and he shall prosper,
Of knowledge and brotherhood he is the master.

48. Half Empty

Somehow these days, there seems like a vacuum,
Everything is present, but unrealisable.
My existence are like a half empty bottle,
Where water is visible, yet so impalpable.
There's so much in my hands,
But like soft sand, slowly slipping.
My heart is overwhelmed and full,
And tears are unnoticeably falling.
Is it time I shall realise god and his being?
Or shall I simply accept this action disgraced?
Shall I question all my flaws?
Or were there issues the way my issues were faced?
This barrenness is eating me up,
I either need explanations or decisions.
There's an urge in me to feel my soul,
And understand all bits of me in precisions.

49. Half Full

In the twilight's hush, where dreams entwine,
A symphony of stars align.
Beneath the moon's ethereal glow,
The tale of "half full" begins to flow.
In whispers sweet, the night confides,
The secrets that the darkness hides.
For in the silence, truths unfold,
In whispers of the young and old.
Half full, the cup of life we hold,
Its stories written, yet untold.
In every sip, a taste of fate,
In every pause, a moment great.
Through valleys deep and mountains high,
We journey 'neath the endless sky.
Half full, the spirit's endless quest,
In every trial, we find our best.
For in the dance of light and shade,
A balance found, a serenade.
In every heart, a spark of fire,
In every soul, a deep desire.
So let us raise our voices high,
To the anthem of the endless sky.
For in the chorus of our song,

Half full, we find where we belong.

50. Half A Century

I've always wondered how my speech,
On my fiftieth birthday, to crowds would reach.
Here I write my imaginary sample,
Hope you all give it love in ample-
In the dance of time, a half century's embrace,
Echoes of moments, each a whispered grace.
Fifty years spun on life's tapestry's loom,
In each thread, memories bloom and gloom,
A journey mapped in joy and in tear's trace.
Through seasons of laughter and storms fierce,
In the heart's chamber, memories pierce.
Golden sunsets and mornings dew-kissed,
In the symphony of life, we persist,
Half a century's tale, no chapter rehearsed.
Dreams painted on the canvas of fate,
Challenges faced, some met too late.
Yet resilience like a river flows,
Through the valleys of highs and lows,
Half a century's wisdom, life's intricate state.
With each passing year, a lesson learned,
In the book of life, pages turned.
Love's enduring flame, a guiding light,
Through the darkest of nights, shining bright,

Half a century's journey, a legacy earned.
So here's to fifty years, a milestone grand,
In the tapestry of life, a golden strand.
With gratitude for the journey's length,
And the treasures found in strength,
Half a century's symphony, hand in hand.

51. Multiple Choice Questions

Sometimes I wish life was trappable,
Presented like multiple choice questions.
Answer simplified in four or six options,
All similar but uncomparable.
And a little elimination, a little choice,
And you've found the answer to your voice.
Analysis of only some paths,
No distress, no wrath, no panic.
Conscientious ideas, display systematic,
Everything narrowed down in footpaths.
When all this seems confusing and whacky,
To resort we have "inky pinky ponky".
Apply knowledge a bit, a bit of experience,
Give your mind limited recourses.
Channelise your character into correct resources.
Seems so simple for so many reasons.
Yet it is appalling, what could be the result,
No personalization, no overthinking cult.

www.ingramcontent.com/pod-product-compliance
Lightning Source LLC
Chambersburg PA
CBHW021119130726
47988CB00003B/1082